PAKISTAN

LETTERS FROM AROUND THE WORLD

David Cumming

Photographs by Julio Etchart

CHERRYTREE BOOKS

LETTERS FROM AROUND THE WORLD

Distributed in the United States by
Cherrytree Books
1980 Lookout Drive
North Mankato, MN 56001

Library of Congress Cataloging-in-Publication Data
Cumming, David, 1953-
    Pakistan / by David Cumming.
      p.cm. – (Letters from around the world)
    Includes index.
    ISBN 1-84234-243-6 (alk. paper)
      1. Pakistan--Juvenile literature. I Title. II. Series.

DS376.9.C858 2004
954.91--dc22
                                           2004041308

First Edition
9 8 7 6 5 4 3 2 1

First published in 2004 by
Evans Brothers Ltd
2A Portman Mansions
Chiltern Street
London W1U 6NR

Conceived and produced by

Nutshell
MEDIA

www.nutshellmedialtd.co.uk

Editor: Polly Goodman
Design: Mayer Media Ltd
Cartography: Encompass Graphics Ltd
Artwork: Mayer Media Ltd
Consultants: Jeff Stanfield and Anne Spiring

All photographs were taken by Julio Etchart,
    except: pp 8 & 29 (left): Jimmy Holmes.

Printed in China

Acknowledgments
The photographer would like to thank the Shah family, the
staff and students of Dheri Naqazchian School, Mian
Dheri, Pakistan, and Waqas Mahmood from the Aga Khan
Foundation, Islamabad, for all their help with this book.

Cover: Tunweer (third from left) with other players from
    his school cricket team. From the left, they are: Ali,
    Wahid, Rafiq, Rahjid, Ghulam, and Mowahid.
Title page: Tunweer carries cut plant food for the goats
    to eat.
This page: Villagers walk along the floodplains of the
    Indus river.
Contents page: Tunweer breaks off a piece of *chapatti*
    to eat.
Glossary page: Tunweer and his brother Zamir walk
    to school.
Further Information page: Tunweer on the batting side of a
    school cricket match.
Index: Tunweer and his friends drinking tea and eating
    chapattis for breakfast.

Contents

My Country

Wednesday, January 8

c/o Hazara Post Office
Punjab Province
Pakistan

Dear Joe,

Assalam alaikum! (pronounced "Ah-sal-um ah-lay-kum." This means "hello" in Urdu, an important language in Pakistan.)

My name is Tunweer Shah and I'm eight years old. I live in the village of Mian Dheri, in northern Pakistan. I have a brother, Zamir, who's seven, and a sister, Sumayya, who's five.

I'm glad I'm going to be your pen pal. I can help you with your class projects on Pakistan.

Write back soon!

From

Tunweer

Here I am (in a white shirt) eating dinner with my mother, brother, and sister.

4

The country that is now Pakistan was only formed in 1947. Before then, it was part of India. In 1971, East Pakistan became a new country, called Bangladesh.

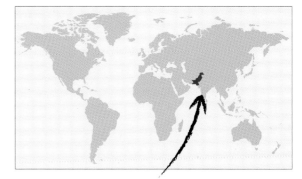

Pakistan's place in the world.

The Karakoram mountains in northern Pakistan are among the highest in the world.

N

0   100   200 kilometers

0   100   200 miles

CHINA

K2
28,484 ft
(8,611 m)
KARAKORAM RANGE

JAMMU & KASHMIR

Indus

Mian Dheri

Peshawar

ISLAMABAD

Rawalpindi

Chenab

PUNJAB   Lahore

Faisalabad

Ravi

Indus

Sutlej

AFGHANISTAN

PAKISTAN

RAN

CENTRAL MAKRAN RANGE

Indus

THAR DESERT

INDIA

Karachi

Arabian Sea

The center of Pakistan is a wide plain called the Punjab. The Punjab means "land of five rivers." It was named after the tributaries of the Indus River, which flow across the plain.

The Punjab is home to most of Pakistan's population. The soil here is good for farming and the rivers provide plenty of water. Most people in the Punjab live in villages like Mian Dheri.

Mian Dheri's houses have flat roofs for storing wood and drying out crops in the sun.

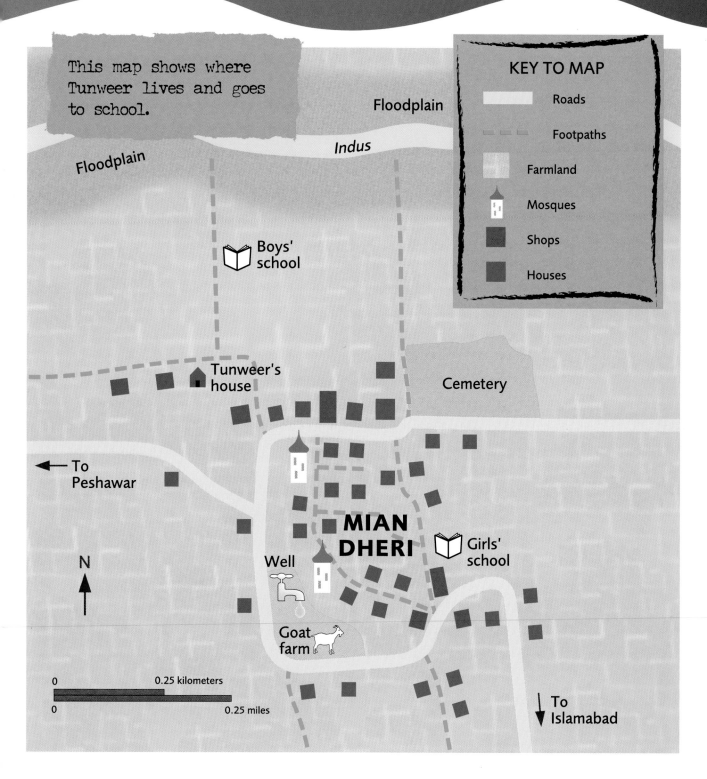

This map shows where Tunweer lives and goes to school.

KEY TO MAP

Roads	
Footpaths	
Farmland	
Mosques	
Shops	
Houses	

Floodplain

Floodplain

Indus

Boys' school

Tunweer's house

Cemetery

To Peshawar

N

MIAN DHERI

Girls' school

Well

Goat farm

0   0.25 kilometers

0   0.25 miles

To Islamabad

Mian Dheri is a large village about 500 yards (0.5 km) from the Indus River. There is no bridge near the village, but when the river is low enough, people can walk across to the other side.

Landscape and Weather

Pakistan has many different landscapes and climates. In the northern mountains, winters are freezing while summers are warm. In the Punjab and southern deserts, there are warm winters and very hot summers.

Much of the Karakoram mountain range is covered with snow all year round.

A southwest wind called the monsoon brings rain in July and August. The rain can cause floods.

Most of Pakistan's food is grown on the fertile floodplains beside the Indus River.

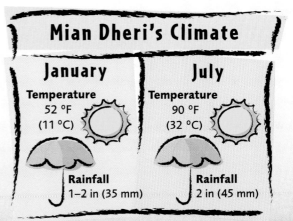

Mian Dheri's Climate

January

Temperature
52 °F
(11 °C)

Rainfall
1–2 in (35 mm)

July

Temperature
90 °F
(32 °C)

Rainfall
2 in (45 mm)

At Home

Tunweer lives in a one-story house made of bricks. It has a flat roof and two big rooms. One of the rooms is the living room. Tunweer's parents sleep in the other room.

A kitchen, bathroom, toilet, and storeroom are in the building next to the house. There is a courtyard in front.

All the houses in Mian Dheri have courtyards like Tunweer's house.

Tunweer, Zamir, and Summaya have beds in the sleeping area of the living room.

There are two trees in the courtyard. Tunweer often sits under their shade to do his homework. There is electricity and running water, but Tunweer's family has little furniture and no electrical equipment, except for a radio.

Tunweer's family gets all its water from this faucet in the courtyard.

Tunweer carries some freshly cut plant food for the goats.

Tunweer's dad keeps cows and goats near the house. He uses them for milk and meat. Tunweer's mom makes some of the milk into cheese and yogurt.

Tunweer and Zamir help to feed the goats. Sumayya helps their mom to keep the house clean and to prepare the meals.

The food is chopped up by a special machine that is powered by electricity. The machine has very sharp blades.

Thursday, February 6

c/o Hazara Post Office
Punjab Province
Pakistan

Assalam alaikum!

Thanks for your letter. We keep animals, too. There are four goats—two adults and their babies. The baby goats are called kids. They follow me around everywhere.

It's my job to feed the goats. Every morning, I cut and gather up a special crop we grow for them. I take it to Mr. Shukat, our neighbor. He's got a machine to chop it up so it's easier for the goats to eat. Do you have any chores?

Write back and tell me.

From

Tunweer

Here I am feeding finely chopped plant food to the goats.

Food and Mealtimes

For breakfast, Tunweer has some bread and jam, with a cup of sweet tea. Lunch is usually lamb or chicken curry, with rice and *chapattis* or nan. The leftovers are heated up for the evening meal, when there is also yogurt and tea.

Tunweer has breakfast with his brother, sister, and three friends.

Tunweer shares a lamb curry for lunch with his father, brother, sister, and cousins.

Tunweer's mother boils some water on the fire in the kitchen.

In Tunweer's home, food is cooked on a wood-burning fire. Tunweer helps his mother collect the wood from nearby. A few families in the village use bottled gas in their kitchens.

Tunweer and his friends Iqbal and Abbas with fruit drinks from a village shop.

Tunweer's family are Muslims. They do not eat any pork because it is forbidden by their religion, Islam. Muslims consider pigs to be dirty. For this reason, there are no pigs in Pakistan.

Tunweer's mom buys food from the village stores. Tunweer and Zamir bring her vegetables from the family's land. A neighbor has a big oven that Tunweer's mom uses to bake bread.

On this street stall, a woman is frying *parathas*. These are thick pancakes that are eaten at breakfast.

Wednesday, March 5

c/o Hazara Post Office
Punjab Province
Pakistan

Hi Joe,

Here's the recipe for *chapattis* that you asked for:

You will need: 2 cups wholemeal flour, sieved; $3/4$ cup water.

1. Put the flour in a bowl and slowly add the water.
2. Knead the dough until it is smooth. Cover with a damp cloth and leave for 30 minutes.
3. Roll the dough into small balls. Put them on to a floured surface and use a rolling pin to make thin pancakes.
4. Heat a frying pan and add one *chapattis*. Cook on a low heat for one minute on either side.
5. Using tongs, lift the *chapattis* and hold it over a low flame or heat for a few seconds, to make it puff up (my mom usually does this bit).

Let me know what you think!

Bye

Tunweer

Here I am with a fresh, warm *chapattis*—great on its own or with food.

School Day

Tunweer and his brother go to the boys' school just across the fields from their home. Sumayya goes to the girls' school, which is on the other side of the village. In Pakistan, girls and boys go to separate schools because this is what is recommended by Islam.

It takes Tunweer and Zamir about 10 minutes to walk to school each day.

At 8 A.M. students line up for assembly in the school playground.

Tunweer's school doesn't have enough money for desks and chairs. The students sit on the floor instead.

Tunweer's school starts at 8 A.M. and finishes at 12:30 P.M. All the boys have to wear the same uniform. It is a dark-gray *salwar khameez*—a long tunic over baggy pants. It is good for keeping cool during the hot summers.

Tunweer's teacher has made a calculator to teach math. He can find answers by adjusting the numbers on the rings.

Tunweer studies two Pakistani languages (Urdu and Punjabi), as well as math, science, and Islam. He plays soccer in the winter and cricket during the summer months.

The school year starts in September, when the monsoon rains have stopped. The two main vacations are during Ramadan, the Muslim holy month, and August.

Tunweer's dad helps him with his homework, sitting on a traditional Pakistani bed.

Tuesday, April 1

c/o Hazara Post Office
Punjab Province
Pakistan

Dear Joe,

So baseball's your favorite sport. Cricket's mine. Everyone here is crazy about it. Pakistan comes to a standstill when there's a game on TV. People crowd outside TV shops or go over to neighbors who own a TV. Like you, I play for the school team. We're the champions in this area. I'm one of the best batsmen, and I led the team in batting last season!

Write soon.

From

Tunweer

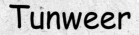

Here's me batting for the cricket team.

Off to Work

Every day, Tunweer's dad ties up his cows to feed and milk them. The cows are also used to pull a plow in the fields or a cart.

Tunweer's dad is a farmer. Apart from goats, he has a small herd of cows that produce the family's milk. He also has some land outside the village for growing vegetables. He grows enough to feed his family, as well as having some left over to sell to people in the village.

This farmer is preparing the soil for planting seeds.

Other farmers in the village grow rice and wheat. There are also metal workers, carpenters, potters, and several tailors. They all have small workshops.

In the cities there are large factories making medical and sports equipment and clothes. Most of these goods are sold to other countries in Europe and North America.

Kites are so popular in Pakistan that making them is big business. These men are dying the lines that are attached to kites.

Free Time

Only the richer families in Mian Dheri have a television. But for most of the year the weather is too good to stay indoors. Like most children in Pakistan, Tunweer and his friends enjoy playing cricket and flying kites.

Atif is best at batting among Tunweer's friends.

At the end of a working day, Tunweer's dad usually meets other farmers to drink tea and chat. His mom likes to go to a friend's house. Her friend has a television and a cassette player.

Tunweer's friend Gulzar makes a kite out of paper and thin bits of wood glued together.

Friday, May 2

c/o Hazara Post Office
Punjab Province
Pakistan

Dear Joe,

What's my favorite hobby? Well, it's cricket again! We don't have a playing field in the village, just a patch of land on the side of the road. We've got a real bat and a ball, but we make the wickets ourselves. They're bits of stick, about the same length, which we put into blocks of mud we've dried in the sun. We don't bother with the crossbars you put on top of the wickets.

From

Tunweer

Here I am putting the finishing touches on the wickets with Shahnaz and Umar.

Religion

Like most people in Pakistan, Tunweer and his family are Muslims. From a very young age, Tunweer was taught to pray five times a day.

At home, Tunweer's dad prays on a raised wooden platform. The others pray on mats on the floor. Each time they pray, they face toward Makkah, in Saudi Arabia. Makkah is the holiest city in Islam.

Tunweer's dad prays on a special rug on the platform at home.

In the *madrasah*, children learn Arabic and read the Qur'an.

On Friday, Islam's holy day, Tunweer goes to the mosque with his dad after school. Afterward he goes to the *madrasah* (the mosque's school), where he learns about the Qur'an. This is the Muslim holy book.

Muslims always leave their shoes outside the mosque to show respect by keeping it clean.

Fact File

Capital City: The capital of Pakistan is Islamabad. It is home to the Shah Faisal mosque, which is the biggest mosque in Pakistan.

Other Major Cities: Karachi, Lahore, Faisalabad, and Rawalpindi.

Size: 309,035 square miles (803,940 km²).

Population: 147,663,429.

History: About 4,500 years ago, one of the world's first civilizations began in the Indus Valley, in what is now called Pakistan. Its capital, Mohenjo-Daro, was very advanced for the time. Since then, the region has been ruled by different peoples.

Flag: The star and crescent on Pakistan's flag are traditional symbols of Islam. The white band on the left of the flag represents the other religions followed in Pakistan.

Languages: Urdu is the national language of Pakistan. English and Punjabi are other important languages.

Currency: Pakistani rupee (divided into paisa). 1 rupee = 100 paisa.

Main Industries: Cotton, food processing, building materials, paper, shrimps.

Main Crop: Wheat is Pakistan's main crop. Cotton, rice, sugarcane, chickpeas, oilseeds, fruits, and vegetables are also important.

Highest mountain: K2, or Mount Godwin-Austen, 28,484 feet (8,611 m).

Longest River: The longest river is the Indus, 1,800 miles (2,900 km).

Main Religions: Islam is the largest religion in Pakistan. About 97 percent of Pakistanis follow it. There are also Christians and Hindus.

Stamps: Pakistani stamps often show famous Pakistanis, the Muslim symbol, or the country's plants.

Glossary

chapatti Thin, round bread that looks like a pancake. It is eaten with curry.

civilization A group of people with a well-organized way of life.

courtyard A small space surrounded by high walls.

curry Food cooked with spices, like chillies, to make it taste hot.

fertile Soil that is good for farming.

flood Water covering land that is usually dry.

floodplain Land beside a river that is flooded when the river overflows.

Islam A major world faith.

monsoon A strong wind that brings rain.

mosque The building in which Muslims pray.

Muslim A follower of Islam.

nan A type of bread, like a very thick pancake, which is eaten at lunch and dinner.

plain A large area of flat land, often beside a river.

population All the people who live in one place: a country, for example.

Ramadan This is the holy month during which Muslims do not eat or drink anything during the daytime.

salwar khameez The traditional dress of Pakistan.

story One whole floor of a building.

tributaries Small rivers that flow into a larger one.

wickets Sticks that are bowled at in a game of cricket.

Further Information

Information books:

Graham, Ian. *Country Files: Pakistan.* Watts, 2003.

Khan, Eaniqa & Unwin, Rob. *Country Insights: Pakistan.* Raintree/Steck-Vaughn, 1998.

Marchant, Kerena. *Festival Tales: Muslim Festivals.* Raintree/Steck-Vaughn, 2001.

Dore, I. *Fiesta!: Pakistan.* Watts, 2001.

Hegedus, Umar. *Keystones: Muslim Mosque.* A&C Black, 2000.

Senker, Cath. *A Year of Religious Festivals: My Muslim Year.* Hodder & Stoughton Children's Division, 2003.

Fiction:

Willis, Clint (ed). *High: Stories of Survival from Everest and K2.* Thunder's Mouth Press, 1999.

Fisher Staples, Suzanne. *Shabanu: Daughter of the Wind.* Random House Children's Books, 1999.

Mathieson, Feroza. *The Very Hot Samosas: A Story Set in Pakistan.* Talman Company, 1991.

Web sites:

CIA Factbook
www.cia.gov/cia/publications/factbook/
Basic facts and figures about Pakistan and other countries.

Index